HE SHOOTS... HE SKEV

ONCE AGAIN, SID OPTED NOT TO SHAKE HANDS.

Published in Canada by Summit Studios • 2010

Library and Archives Canada Cataloguing in Publication

Duncan, Randy, 1963-
He shoots-- he skewers! / Randy Duncan.

ISBN 978-0-9734671-9-2

1. Hockey players--Caricatures and cartoons. 2. National Hockey
League--Caricatures and cartoons. 3. Hockey--Caricatures and cartoons.
4. Canadian wit and humor, Pictorial. I. Title.

NC1449.D78A4 2010   796.962'640207   C2010-904983-7

Illustrations: Randy Duncan
Writing: Randy Duncan and Michael Somma
Designed by MB&S Design
Printed and Bound in Canada

We're very proud of this book. Let us know what you think at r.duncan@rogers.com

To place an order, please visit www.summitstudios.biz.

CONTENTS

INTRODUCTION

Like most Canadians growing up, hockey played an important role in surviving the long, cold winter months. If I wasn't playing pick-up with family or friends at an outdoor rink or pond, my parents were driving me to minor league games. And if I wasn't playing the game, I was watching it on television. In other words, I ate, breathed and slept hockey, which might help explain my grades at school and why I've put together this book instead of teaching or practicing medicine or law.

Even today, most of my closest acquaintances are avid fans. I'm fortunate in this respect because it's given me the opportunity to pick the minds of hockey aficionados for concepts to compliment, and sometimes contradict, my own. In fact I'll subject almost anyone to my ideas, be it a stranger in a bar or a friend when the conversation has hit a lull. Often my brother's laugh or look of bewilderment would be the barometer by which my caricatures measured up, or not… I saw a lot of bewilderment. Two co-workers, Alan and Cameron, have also been a great source to tap. Like myself, Alan likes to throw ideas out there and we've collaborated on more than a few occasions.

But it's been my family that has provided the most support. One might expect their parents to be supportive, but mine have gone far beyond the call of duty. My brother-in-law, a Blackhawks fan in Habs territory, has provided endless hours of advice and design expertise, making this collection possible. When my writing skills were found wanting, enter my nephew and co-writer, Michael. He's quick with a word and good with a pen (or keyboard these days). Just like a hockey team, each brought their own skill-set to the table and together, like a clean tic-tac-toe play, we've netted a winner.

CROSBY, STAALS, NASH AND... OVECHKIN?

Crosby, Staals and Nash and they're all young! Ok, we're not talking about 1970s rock super-group CSN, but the NHL is glad these youngsters have emerged to replace the Gretzkys, Lemieuxs and Yzermans of yesterday. Crosby has quickly risen to the top of the charts, Nash is scoring like a band member and the multiple Staals are no longer appearing solely on account of drug hallucinations. With brothers Eric, Marc and Jordan already in the league, and younger sibling Jared on the way, they really are multiplying! These young stars have the future of the NHL looking bright. Here's hoping they keep churning out hits (and goals) for many years to come.

Number one draft pick Sidney Crosby exceeds high expectations and supplants Dale Hawerchuk as the youngest player to reach 100 points. Despite Crosby's heroics, the Penguins would still finish in the Eastern Conference cellar.

With three brothers and a possible fourth on the way, the Staals still can't compete
with the Sutter family record of six siblings in the NHL.

After signing on as a brand ambassador for an online poker company, Mats Sundin was lured back to the NHL by an extravagant contract offer from the Canucks. Unfortunately a successful return wasn't in the cards, as Mats' performance folded under pressure.

Blackhawk teammates and Calder trophy rivals, Jonathan Toews and Patrick Kane.

Continuing the tradition of Pittsburgh Penguin scoring champions, sophomore Sidney Crosby cashes in on his Art Ross and MVP awards by signing a 5 year contract extension, making him the highest paid player in hockey. If he follows mentor Mario Lemieux's footsteps, it won't be long before the Pens go bankrupt again and he assumes ownership of the team.

Alexander Ovechkin nets 52 goals in his rookie season, including a spectacular effort while sliding on his back.

TALE OF THE TAPE

ALEX OVECHKIN

AGE · 21

SEX · MALE

PROFESSION·
HOCKEY PLAYER

HIGHLIGHTS·
"THERE ARE
VIDEOTAPES OF
ME SCORING
ON MY BACK"

PARIS HILTON

AGE · 26

SEX ·"YES PLEASE"

PROFESSION·
~~TRAMP~~
~~SOCIALITE~~
TRAMP

HIGHLIGHTS·
"LIKE HE SAID,
BEING VIDEOTAPED
ON MY BACK!
DUH!"

6'
5'6
5'
4'6
4'
3'6
3'

Peter Cusimano, the owner of a local Michigan fish market, started the tradition of throwing an octopus onto the ice back in 1952. Each of the eight tentacles represented a win on the way to a championship. Despite the lack of sixteen tentacle octopuses, the tradition continues today before the opening face-off or after a Detroit goal.

With two stars of equal caliber, most teams will choose the lesser of the two contracts.
Dany Heatley earned $4.5 million, Hossa earned $6 mil. Exit Marian Hossa.

Ottawa's savings plan was soon quashed, as consecutive 50 goal seasons netted
Dany Heatley a contract extension worth $7.5 million annually.

When the Boston Red Sox traded Babe Ruth to the New York Yankees in 1920, it was 86 years before they were crowned champions again. When the Boston Bruins traded Joe Thornton in 2005-06, they became the only team to trade a player during the season in which he was named MVP. Will Boston suffer though another Bambino-like curse? This might be more relevant if they weren't already mired in a 30+ year Cup-less drought.

Rookie of the year, Evgeni Malkin.

Rocket Richard Trophy recipient Rick Nash and NBA MVP Steve Nash.

Canada's Simon Gagne and Sweden's Peter Forsberg enjoy great chemistry together in Philadelphia before joining their respective national teams for the 2006 Olympic games.

Pavel Datsyuk, a 6th round selection in 1998, headlines the group of players replacing longstanding, respected veterans in Detroit. The fact that the team scarcely missed a beat is a tribute to their world-class scouting staff, who successfully uncovered late round gems such as Datsyuk, Henrik Zetterberg (7th round, 1999) and Tomas Holmstrom (10th round, 1994).

Without a shred of evidence to back it up, head of the World Anti-doping Agency Dick Pound suggests a third of NHL players could test positive for performance enhancers. Forget drugs, the league's real problem is the lack of respect the players show for one another.

Twins Daniel and Henrik Sedin with ex-playmate Pam Anderson.

DRINKING FROM LORD STANLEY'S CUP... EEEEWWWW.

1959 MVP Andy Bathgate couldn't do it. Jean Ratelle, Rod Gilbert and Brad Park together couldn't do it either. Winning a Stanley Cup at any time with any team is tough enough, but for 54 years, winning in New York was near impossible. It took that long for a player talented and resourceful enough to lead a Ranger team to victory. That player was of course hockey's greatest leader, Mark Messier.

Messier was born to be a New Yorker. He enjoyed the spotlight and on the ice he'd done more than his share of muggings. There were rumors he dated Madonna, and he had the resources to please the material girl if he did. He also made bold predictions of victory a la Joe Namath, and backed it up with a come from behind, third period hat trick against New Jersey in the 1994 semi-finals. But most importantly he followed that up with the Stanley Cup winning goal in game 7 of the finals over Vancouver, becoming the first player to captain two different teams to championships.

Dave Keon and the Leafs celebrated with their 4th Cup of the decade in 1967.

They haven't won it since.

ORR, ESPOSITO AND THE REST OF THE BRUINS
KNEW IT WAS OVER WHEN THE FAT LADY SANG!

With 15 goals, the speedy Yvan Cournoyer was the 1973 Conn Smythe winner.

For Montreal Canadien stalwarts Jacques Lemaire, Guy Lapointe and Bob Gainey, winning the Stanley Cup became a rite of spring during the 1970's.
They drank from the Cup six times, including four in a row, '76-'79.

After being traded to Colorado, Patrick Roy added two Cups to go with the pair he won in Montreal. The Canadiens have had very little success since.

FLIP SIDE

POST CARD

COLORADO AVALANCHE

LES CANADIENS
MOLSON CENTER
1275 St. ANTOINE St.
MONTREAL QUEBEC H3C 5L2

HELLO CANADIENS, I'M SOOOO HOT HERE IN COLORADO! YOU KNOW HOW IT IS PLAYING AT THIS TIME OF YEAR?! OOOPS,

MAYBE NOT. I WON'T KEEP YOU FROM TEE OFF TIME, I'VE GOT TO GOOOAL NA NA NA NA, NA NA NA NA, AY AY AY GOOD-BYE XOXOXO'S ST. PATRICK

Led by veterans like Bryan Trottier, the N.Y. Islanders won their fourth consecutive Cup in 1983, sweeping the young, inexperienced Edmonton Oilers.

N.Y. ISLANDER VERSION OF BRASS KNUCKLES

Gretzky's wizardry with the puck led to four Stanley Cup rings.

Jeremy Roenick and Patrick Roy engage in a battle of wits during the 1996 playoffs.

In the 2007 Stanley Cup finals Ottawa couldn't match Anaheim's shooting skills and occasionally were caught shooting at the wrong target.

Q • WHY DID ALFIE SHOOT AT SCOTT?

A • HE SAW A WILD ANIMAL ATTACKING HIS FACE.

Ryan Smyth and Chris Pronger were important contributors to the Oilers surprising run to the 2006 Finals. Little did Edmonton fans know, both players would be traded away in less than a year's time.

Even opponents were happy to see Lanny McDonald win his first Stanley Cup with the '89 Flames.

I THOUGHT I HAD ONE IN ME!

"I always tell Bobby he was up in the air for so long that I had time to shower and change before he hit the ice."
– Blues goalie Glenn Hall on Bobby Orr's famous Stanley Cup winning goal in 1970.

THE RUSSIANS ARE COMING, BREAK OUT THE SMIRNOFF.

The Russians are coming! The Russians are…what in hell are the Russians coming for? Are they coming to play our professional hockey players? They're amateurs. We have Bobby Orr! Bobby Orr is hurt? No matter, we have Bobby Hull! Bobby Hull signed with the WHA and won' be asked to play? Uh, oh! The Russians are coming! The Russians are coming!

This type of panic never entered the psyche of the Canadian nation. Even without two of it's biggest stars, a never in doubt attitude prevailed within the Canadian camp, the media and especially the fans. In an eight game series it wasn't questioned whether or not Canada would win, but by how much they'd win each game.

When Team Canada quickly went up 2-0 in game one, the series was simply unfolding the way it was supposed to. The 7-3 final score in favor of the opposition was more of an unraveling. But after 8 heart pounding, nail biting games, Canada had proved it's superiority... and with 34 seconds to spare!

The team had come back from near impossible odds, overcoming a 3-1-1 series deficit by winning the final three games, and they did it in Russia to boot. In the end, it was unsettling for Canadians to learn we were no longer alone atop the hockey world, but even worse would we ever learn to pronounce those Russian names?

Valeri Kharlamov

31

Few Canadians knew his name before the '72 Summit Series, fewer still could forget it after. Vladislav Tretiak starred against Canada and in future international events, eventually becoming the first European inducted into the Hockey Hall of Fame.

TRETIAK MADE IT CLEAR THERE WOULD BE REPERCUSSIONS FOR BEATING HIM DURING THE COLD WAR

After exchanging gifts that included Russian dolls, the Soviets surprised a sluggish Ken Dryden and Team Canada, with a 7-3 victory in Game 1.

Trailing by a goal midway through the third period of Game 8 in Russia, Canada's Yvan Cournoyer scored what appeared to be the equalizer. When the goal light didn't flash on, a livid Alan Eagleson tried to reach the goal judge to show his displeasure but was escorted away by security. Led by Pete Mahovlich, all of Team Canada came to the rescue of 'the Eagle.' Had the Canadian players known then what they knew years later, they would likely have let the Russian military clip his wings.

EAGLESON LEARNS RUSSIAN ROULETTE

Leaders of their respective clubs, Phil Esposito and Boris Mikhailov. Before The Summit Series, it was believed by some journalist that Esposito needed Bobby Orr. By series end, Phil's talents and leadership skills were no longer in doubt.

Veteran Soviet stars Igor Larionov and Vladimir Krutov's careers went in opposite directions after arriving in the NHL in 1989. While Larionov went on to a distinguished NHL career, Krutov's fork in the road led directly to a fork in the mouth. He lacked the self-discipline to keep physically fit for the rigors of a long NHL season.

Speedy Sergei Makarov, a 9-time Soviet scoring champ, was named NHL Rookie of the Year after joining the Calgary Flames in 1989.

After playing 13 years for the Russian Red Army and the National Team under demanding coach Viktor Tikhonov, Viacheslav Fetisov joined the New Jersey Devils in 1989. Apparently he preferred the devil on his jersey to the devil behind the bench.

Alexander Mogilny admitted to a fear of flying and disliking Buffalo.

Pavel Bure was nicknamed the "Russian Rocket" for his speed and dazzling moves, but his defensive abilities left something to be desired.

Ic·a·rus. the son of Yetookoff, Icarus escaped from Russia with wings made by glasnost. After flying into America, Icarus was soon grounded with a severe case of Buffalo-phobia.

*ICARUS TRANSLATED IS MOGILNY

Sergei Fedorov with tennis pal Anna Kournikova.

VALERI KAMENSKY'S EARLY YEARS WERE OFTEN SPENT ON THE
DISABLED LIST DUE TO SAVAGE BATTLES WITH HIS ARCH NEMESIS!

ILLEGAL BORDER CROSSING? Son of Canadian hockey legend Bobby Hull, dual citizen Brett plays for the American squad in the 1996 World Cup and leads them to victory over Canada.

Mike Modano.

CZECHMATE Wayne Gretzky and Team Canada lose their chance at Olympic Gold in 1998, falling 2-1 in a shoot out to the eventual tournament champions, the Czech Republic. A gold medal was one of the few glories that eluded Gretzky as a player.

LEAFS WIN! ... ? Big goals were hard to come by for post-1967 Leaf stars, as they didn't find themselves playing in very many important games. But given the chance, Paul Henderson became a hero for Canada with game winners in the final three games of the '72 Summit Series. Ironically, it was Toronto teammate Darryl Sittler (who babysat Paul's children during the '72 series) that would score the '76 Canada Cup winning goal in overtime.

WE SAVE OUR BEST GOALS FOR TEAM CANADA.... JUST TO PISS OFF HAROLD.

CANADA'S CUP Being compared to Bobby Orr would be a great honor for any player, except for Denis Potvin, who saw second best as the first loser. He certainly acted like a sore loser after a strong '76 Canada Cup performance that he felt merited him MVP, led him to demand; "Is Bobby Orr only going to have to play to be known as the best defenseman?"

NO MIRACLES ON ICE, WE'RE SUPPOSED TO WIN.

With few exceptions we don't star in soccer, baseball or basketball, we're Canadians and we play hockey. We have 2 official languages, so when we say we're the best, Lemieux is an exclamation point! If we don't win, it's the ref's fault because maple Leafs don't just fall, they're tripped. When Bobby Clarke gets a little sticky, blame it on the maple syrup. And we don't have just one Bobby, so if you ignore the others, to Hull with you. Leave our Canadian beaver alone and our Moose won't Mess with you. If you're an opponent and you didn't laugh at the Wayne & Shuster Show, you won't find the Wayne & Mario Show funny either. In the end when Canadians drink, we drink from a dirty Cup and we like our Brodeur strong to the last shot.

Mike Peca.

Olympic figure skater Jamie Salé and Eric Brewer.

Theo Fleury.

Ryan Smyth.

Mario Lemieux and Steve Yzerman were natural choices to lead Canada to its first Olympic gold in 50 years.

Mario, playing alongside Wayne Gretzky in the '87 Canada Cup, upped his game to new heights while leading Canada with 11 goals. Injuries kept him out of future international events, nearly sabotaging his appearance at the 2002 Olympics as well.

A quiet leader, Yzerman wasn't at 100% either. Essentially playing on one leg, Steve followed another great Red Wing, Gordie Howe, and let his actions and determination do his talking for him.

Chris Pronger.

Paul Kariya, Simon Gagné and Olympic speed skater Catrina Lemay Doan.

THE FACE-OFF SPECIALIST

Brendan Shanahan and Owen Nolan.

Cassie Campbell captained Canada's women team to two consecutive Olympic gold medals. The men were less successful in their aim for the gold in 2006.

WHY DID THE WOMEN'S OLYMPIC TEAM DO BETTER THAN THE MEN'S?

NICE COACHES FINISH LAST.

According to Scotty Bowman, "the better coaching has become, the worse the game has become." Well, thanks a lot Scotty. In a career that spanned over five decades, Bowman stands as the most successful coach in NHL history, having led a record 9 teams to Cup championships.

No one could argue with the end results of Scotty's run as coach of the Canadiens (5 Stanley Cups in 8 seasons), but his direct, no nonsense approach didn't endear him to his players. Reflecting on this time, Steve Shutt later had this to say about him: "You hated him 364 days of the year, and on the 365th day you got your Stanley Cup ring."

Love him or hate him, players bought into his system because it worked. He went on to win additional Cups in Pittsburgh and Detroit. In fact, after St Louis, his first head coaching job, the only place he failed to win was Buffalo, and let's face it, NOBODY wins anything in Buffalo.

It's fitting that Scotty's career ended by going where no coach had gone before; parading around the rink in skates with the Cup above his head after Detroit's victory in 2002. Had he tried that stunt in Montreal, one of his players might have checked him through the boards. In the end his players not only respected him, but were smiling along with him.

PHEW! HAS THERE BEEN EXTRA LAYERS ADDED?

ON THE CUP, OR SCOTTY?

Rare is it that a star player can translate their on-ice success to the coaching ranks. Someone should have mentioned that to Toe Blake! After enjoying a decorated career that included a Memorial Cup, a Hart Trophy, an Art Ross trophy as well as three Stanley Cups, Toe joined the coaching ranks with his longtime club, the Canadiens. There he would go on to capture eight more Cup titles, including a record five straight between 1956-1960. As if that wasn't enough, in 1952 he opened "Toe Blake's Tavern" in downtown Montreal, which stayed open until 1983. Not only did he drink from the Stanley Cup on eleven occasions, he provided the champagne for many fans celebrating along with him! What more could Montrealers ask of him?

Punch Imlach coached "the over the hill gang" to Toronto's last Cup in '67.

iT'S TRUE! iT DOES GET EASIER WITH EACH DELIVERY! —

Some coaches like the 'spin-a-rama' as was the case with Bowman and the reliable Serge Savard.

Mike Keenan on the other hand, did not.

Keenan was nicknamed 'Captain Hook', and a few other names that can't be printed.

Mike Milbury may be best known for an altercation he had with Ranger fans while he was a Boston Bruin. Tapes reveal him climbing into the stands and hitting a man with his own shoe. On NBC's telecast with Pierre McGuire it looks like there's enough tension between the two for Mike to revisit the shoe incident.

Pierre McGuire's infatuation with talented junior stars reached new heights when Carey Price backstopped Team Canada to the U-20 World Championship in 2007.

Having coached Boston to its first Cup in 29 years, Harry Sinden quit in 1970 due to a salary dispute with notoriously cheap Bruins management. Ironically, being frugal was the same criticism levelled against Sinden after he returned to the Bruins as GM a short time later. Despite beginning a run of 30 consecutive playoff appearances, his refusal to shell out the big bucks hindered the Bruins chances of winning the Cup.

EVERYBODY LOVES RAYMOND...

HARRY'S ANOTHER STORY!

Sinden finally provides Ray Bourque a supporting cast good enough to win it all… with the Colorado Avalanche.

RAY, WE'RE HONOURING YOUR REQUEST FOR A TRADE,... BECAUSE FRANKLY, WE DON'T WANT TO FORK OUT THE DOUGH FOR A GOLD WATCH IF YOU STAY!

Coach Jacques Martin didn't like his players such as Chris Neil dropping the gloves. This lack of toughness and physical play contributed to early playoff exits. Martin was fired in 2004. He left without a fight.

In a tell all book, Jacques Demers admits he's functionally illiterate, while Saku Koivu , after suffering through a serious eye injury faced French language issues.

Critics call the controversial Don Cherry boisterous, contemptuous, egotistical, feisty, headstrong, intolerant, loud, outspoken, relentless, politically incorrect …etc, etc, etc. But his statements have often proven true, and more often than not, especially during the neutral zone trap era, he was as entertaining as the game itself.

Bobby Orr played only one full year with Cherry as his coach. He won the Norris, the Pearson and Art Ross trophies while scoring 135 points and compiling a league best +80. Simply put, "The greatest hockey player who ever lived, Bobby Orr, and I love him!" – Don Cherry.

Don was often caught on camera, kissing his two favorite players, Bobby Orr and Doug Gilmour. This might help explain some of Don's outfits.

CORNERED, DOUG HAD NO CHOICE BUT TO LET THE KISSING BANDIT HAVE HIS WAY!

During The Battle of Ontario, Don upset Ottawa backers by openly cheering for Toronto.

Labatt replaces Molson as the main sponsor of 'Hockey Night in Canada.'

The CBC decided to use a 7 second delay on Coach's Corner after some controversial remarks by Don and a certain incident during the Super Bowl, when Janet Jackson "accidentally" bares her breast.

MAYBE WE DO NEED A 7 SECOND DELAY

"THIS **CAPS** OFF ANOTHER EDITION OF COACH'S CORNER WHERE DON'S ALL **TAPPED OUT**! NO NO NO! i GOT iT, i GOT iT! DON REFUSES TO TURN **BLUE** ABOUT BEING **CANADIAN**!"

CHASING THE ROCKET, BECAUSE IT'S THE SAFEST PLACE TO BE.

A March 23rd playoff game in 1944 best describes Rocket Richard's scoring exploits. In a 5-1 defeat of Toronto, the Rocket scored all 5 goals for the Canadiens. Imagine the shock in the crowd when the customary 3 star selection is announced in reverse order and " tonight's third star…number 9, Maurice Richard" is heard! Only after hearing "Tonight's second star… number 9, Maurice Richard" did the crowd comprehend the unique honor bestowed upon their explosive star. Maurice had received all 3 stars. The Richard legend was born.

From the blue line in, The Rocket was as scary as OJ on the loose at night. According to goalie Glenn Hall "When he was coming down on you, the puck glued to the end of the stick, his eyes were flashing and gleaming like the lights of a pinball machine. It was frightening." This intensity helped the Rocket to score 544 regular season goals and another 82 in the playoffs, including 6 over time winners. All of these were records at the time.

Maurice was also the first to score 50 goals in 50 games, still considered a benchmark for all snipers. Only Gretzky, Lemieux and Brett Hull have bettered this mark. Is it any wonder why they named a trophy after him for top goal-scorer.

69

Gordie Howe could do it all. He was a play-maker, a sniper and didn't need an enforcer to take care of his dirty work, preferably doing so himself with his elbows. He even had a sense of humor. On the 'Dick Cavett Show,' when asked why he wouldn't wear a helmet, but nonetheless wore a protective cup, a grinning Howe answered "You can always get somebody to do your thinking for you."

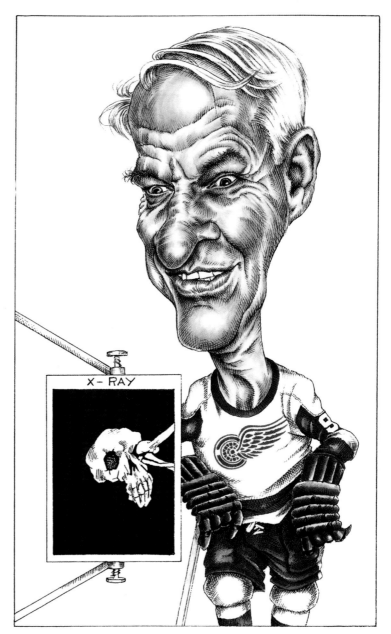

WE BELIEVE WE FOUND THE REASON FOR THE SWELLING MR. HOWE!

Wayne Gretzky's 122 playoff goals marks him as the top post-season goal-scorer of all-time. However during the Oilers' run of four Cups in five years, it was his line-mate, Jari Kurri who was the top scorer, with Gretzky as his set-up man.

Janet Jones.

Bobby Orr considered Mario the most talented player of all-time: "What he can do, I couldn't. He can do more things than any other player I've seen." Never were Orr's words better evidenced than while observing Lemieux score at a record breaking pace during the 1992-93 season. Despite missing two months after being diagnosed with Hodgkin's disease, Mario was still only 12 points behind scoring leader Pat Lafontaine when he made an amazing return to the ice. He would go on to capture the Art Ross and his 2.67 points per game is the third highest single season average of all-time.

Not as prolific a goal-scorer as his arch rival the Rocket, Gordie Howe more than made up for it with his consistency. Gordie scored 20 or more goals for 22 consecutive seasons, finishing with 801.

Even though Howe was Wayne Gretzky's idol growing up, he showed no mercy attacking his all-time records.

Montreal thought so much of youngster Jean Beliveau that they bought the entire Quebec Senior Hockey League in order to secure his services. The talented and classy center was worth every penny.

"Boom-Boom" Geoffrion invented the slapshot, earning his nickname as a result of his thunderous misses off the backboards. However, he did hit the net often enough to become the second player to net 50 in a season.

Punch Imlach drove the Maple Leafs to four Stanley Cups during the 1960's. He also drove his one legitimate goal-scorer, Frank Mahovlich, to a nervous breakdown, and subsequently, out of town.

Slotman Phil Esposito was the first to record a 100 point season in 1969, finishing with 126. Two years later he went on a goal-a-game rampage, smashing the single season record with 76 goals in 78 games.

Wilt Chamberlain scored 100 points in a single NBA game.

Brett surpasses his father's NHL goal totals.

When Bobby Hull signed his million-dollar contract to play in the WHA, he brought legitimacy to the new league. Not surprisingly, he dominated as well. Teaming with Swedish stars Anders Hedberg and Ulf Nilsson in 1975, Hull set a new professional record with 77 goals at the age of 36.

Guy Lafleur and Marcel Dionne were junior stars who went 1-2 in the 1971 draft. The difference between going #1 and #2? Lafleur accumulated six Stanley Cups with the Habs while Dionne's teams struggled for respectability.

WITH YEARS OF HOCKEY ON A CELLAR DWELLER AHEAD, MARCEL DIONNE WOULD EVENTUALLY REGRET CHANGING MARGARINES ON THAT FATEFUL DAY!

Once the helmet came off and Lafleur let his hair down, he terrorized NHL goalies with six consecutive 50 goal seasons.

One of the purest scorers to ever lace up a pair of skates, Mike Bossy recorded nine consecutive 50 goal seasons to begin his career, only falling short of the mark in an injury-riddled year that would prove to be his last. In 1980-81 both he and the Kings' Charlie Simmer took a run at the Rocket's record of 50 goals in 50 games. After Simmer came up just short in an afternoon game, recording a hat trick to tally 49, Bossy fired home two goals that night to match Richard's fantastic feat. He did so despite garnering extra media scrutiny after publicly admitting his pursuit of the record part way through the season.

Teemu Selanne and Paul Kariya were a great 1-2 punch for the Mighty Ducks, but unfortunately the punch of the rest of the team was unspiked.

Jaromir Jagr on Lemieux: "He's the best, he's unbelievable. I try to do some of the things he does in practice."
He did more than just try, as he followed up Mario's scoring titles with five of his own.

The Tampa Bay Lightning duo of Marty St. Louis and Vincent Lecavalier feed off each other as linemates, pushing each to their limits. St. Louis was never given much of a chance on account of his diminutive stature. Listed at 5' 9", though he may have been wearing platform shoes when that measurement was taken, Martin had a break out season in 2003 and followed that up with an MVP caliber year as the Lightning capped off the season with a Stanley Cup.

On the other hand, there were high expectations for Lecavalier when he entered the league, and even more so after Lightning owner, Art Williams proclaimed that Lecavalier would be "the Michael Jordan of hockey." He showed flashes of brilliance early in his career but it wasn't until he played the role of Jean Beliveau in the film 'The Rocket' that he reached his full potential. Vincent donned Beliveau's number 4 to honor him, but is now playing like Big Jean and scoring like the Rocket as he wrapped up his 2007 season by collecting the Maurice Richard Trophy.

In 2002 the Calgary Flames' scoring champion Jarome Iginla was the player's choice as MVP, but had little support.
The Flames missed the playoffs and he missed out on the Hart by a single vote.

With defenseman Mike Green scoring at a frenzied pace, teammate Alex Ovechkin could afford to take some time to work on his goal celebrations. It's too bad his moves and his fashion sense aren't as hot as the stick he wields.

THE TOOLS OF IGNORANCE...AND THE EQUIPMENT THEY WEAR.

They had faces only a coach could love. Quick and agile, they stood fearlessly in defence of their goal, leaving their heads exposed. All-time shutout leader Terry Sawchuck had over 400 stitches on his face, Gerry Cheevers mask may have been as equally scarred. Fortunately, Jacques Plante believed stitching was for tuques, which he did in his spare time.

So why not wear a mask? According to goalie Gump Worsley, "Anyone who wears one is chicken. My face is my mask." But after taking a particularly nasty shot to the face, courtesy of an Andy Bathgate backhander, Jacques Plante refused to return to the ice without protection.

The face of goaltending had changed forever.

LUMPY GUMPY SAT UP ON A POLE
LUMPY GUMPY FLOPPED TO SAVE A GOAL
ALL THE GAME'S REFS AND ALL THE OPPOSING MEN
DECIDED THEY'D NEVER LET GUMPY DO THAT AGAIN

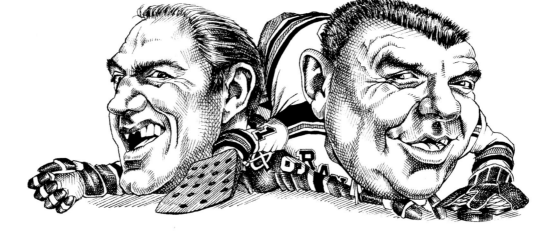

When asked which team gave him the most trouble, New York's Gump Worsley smartly replied, "The Rangers." Jacques Plante soon discovered just how true these words were when he joined the team following a swap that sent Gump to the Canadiens. A defiant Plante claimed he'd still win a 7th Vezina trophy for top goalie, but after two rough seasons he announced his retirement, fed up with the woeful team in front of him.

MONTREAL TRADES PLANTE TO N.Y.

Turk Broda is regarded as one of the NHL's all time clutch goalies. His regular season goals against average of 2.53 plummeted to 1.98 come playoff time, and because of this he had 5 cups under his belt. Unfortunately that wasn't all he was hiding there. Apparently Broda not only drank from the cup but ate from it as well.

Terry Sawchuk's career choice may have been summed up best by fellow goaltender Gump Worsley. Never at a loss for words the Gumper suggested that "the only job worse is a javelin catcher at a track & field meet." While Terry is regarded by many experts as the greatest goalie ever, recording 103 shutouts, he also suffered numerous shots to his face, had stress related depression and died in an off ice altercation with a teammate. In hindsight catching javelins might have been easier.

JOHNNY KNEW THAT STAN, A CZECHOSLOVAKIAN NATIVE WAS NOW CANADIAN
BUT HE COULDN'T HELP HIMSELF, THE POKE-CHECK WAS HIS BEST MOVE.

He had an iron man streak of 502 straight games, recorded 84 career shutouts and in 1961 led Chicago to it's first cup in 23 years. They've not won it since! All of this while being sick to his stomach before most games or between periods leaving a team-mate to suggest "some day Hall's bucket should be in the hall of fame." Glenn himself was elected in 1975.

GLENN HALL HATED PRE-GAME WARM-UPS!

Tony and brother Phil Esposito.

Gerry Cheevers marked his mask indicating where he would have been scarred by pucks or sticks had he not been wearing it.

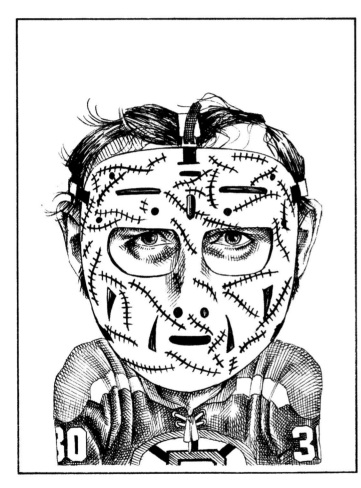

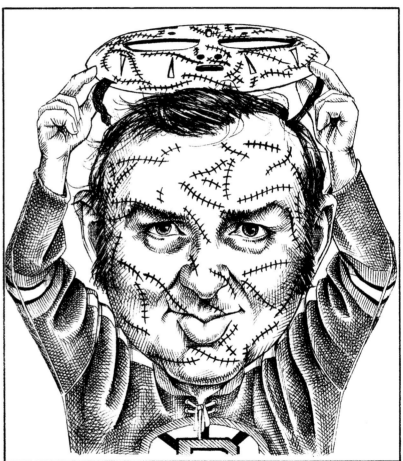

With the Habs down in third, and almost in ruins
  They would now have to face the big bad Bruins

Then a lawman arrived, he'd been to McGill
  As fans would soon learn, he'd give them a thrill

Replacing Rogie Vachon, the king of French cake
  Media and fans alike, called it a mistake

Ken rested on his stick, having no previous laurels
  With these angry Bruins he'd soon be in quarrels

Led by Espo, Bucyk and the great Bobby Orr
  Their attack had no quit, it kept coming for more

But with limbs like an octopus and a very quick hand
  The lawman named Dryden was making his stand

As the clock ticked down and with victory in sight
  The concerns had been quelled about the feared Bruin bite

On his way to the Smythe, among the riches he'd reap
  The Bruins were tamed, for Dryden to keep

Rogie Vachon was once considered the heir to Montreal's goaltending throne, but some inconsistent play combined with Ken Dryden's quick accession relegated the diminutive keeper to the end of the bench. After being granted his request for a trade, Rogie was once again on his way to being a "King"…albeit in Los Angeles.

WHAT CAN A GANGLY ROOKIE DO THAT A LIGHTNING QUICK, OOOPS MISSED THAT ONE, SEASONED VET CAN'T?

If Bobby Clarke was Philly's inspiration during their Cup runs, then Bernie Parent was their opponents exasperation. The first player to win back-to-back Conn Smythe trophies as playoff MVP, his post-season performances in 1974-75 inspired the bumper sticker "only the Lord saves more than Bernie Parent."

Hack and Slash

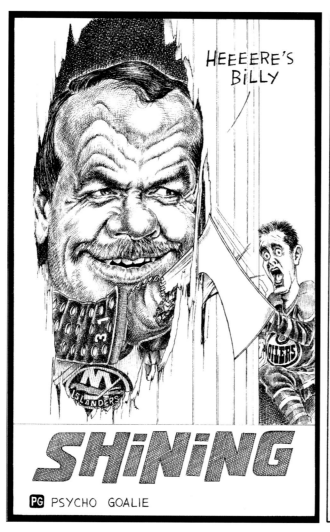

Curtis Joseph's nickname "Cujo" came from the use of the first two letters of his name. It also accurately describes the tenaciousness of his goaltending.

…but Martin Brodeur finished it in 2002.

Dallas parted ways with all star Ed Belfour when his name became more prominent in police reports than score sheets. The more affordable Marty Turco filled the void left in goal by setting a modern NHL record with a 1.72 goals against average the next year.

Hasek's heroics brought Buffalo within a foot of the Cup in '99.

Roy's showboating during game 6 of the 2002 Conference Finals against Detroit cost Colorado a shot at repeating as champions.

Ottawa's John Muckler thought he'd pulled a fast one on the rest of the league when he signed 41 year old all star Dominik "the Dominator" Hasek…

…but the only thing pulled was an adductor muscle.

Dominik Hasek and Senators/horse owner Eugene Melnyk

Does sIze matter?

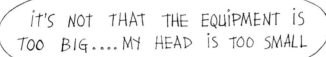

Through 341 games with the New York Islanders and the Florida Panthers, Roberto Luongo's teams had never qualified for a playoff game.

THE GOOD, THE BAD AND THE JUST PLAIN UGLY.

One of the more storied franchises in NHL history, Toronto dominated the '40s and '60s, winning 9 of their 13 Stanley Cups. An impressive run, but it's been countered by some trying times since. In fact, they haven't even been to the final after the league's original expansion… in 1967!

No, this isn't about the last 40+ years of Maple Leaf hockey. There have been many more unfortunate or disturbing events that have taken place in the NHL to focus solely on the fortunes of the Leafs.

Occurrences like Alan Eagleson siphoning funds from the players union that he helped to create; the Richard Riot in Montreal; Todd Bertuzzi being well… Todd Bertuzzi; and Alexei Yashin's shenanigans left a bad taste in the mouths of Senators' fans and possibly girlfriend Carol Alt's as well.

Despite all that, the Maple Leafs still get the headliner page, because nothing could be uglier than the Ballard years in Toronto.

Leaf legends Syl Apps, Ted Kennedy and George Armstrong pass grand tradition to Harold Ballard. With him as majority owner, Toronto had only six winning seasons out of 18.

THAT'S GOOD! NO, THAT'S BAD!

The Nordiques had a great team through the 80's and that was good.
No, that was bad. In their quest for success they aged and finished the 1991 season in last.

But in finishing last, they drafted number one, and that was good.
No that was bad. Lindros was the pick and his mommy said no to La Belle Province.

But the Nordiques traded Eric to N.Y. for many good players, and that was good.
No that was bad because they also traded him to Philly for more, at the very same time

But the league ruled against N.Y. and Quebec got Forsberg and that was good
No that was bad. While Peter was great, he didn't solve their problem in goal.

But the Nords rose near the top, led by Peter and Joe and that was good.
No that was bad because without goaltending they didn't win and moved west in an Avalanche.

But now out of Quebec, they netted Saint Patrick in a trade, and that was good.
No that was bad. They finally won it all, but the team was no longer their own.

But in the end Lindros didn't win, the headaches were his own and Quebecers thought, "Phew, at least that was good."

While Ballard served jail time for fraud and grand theft, the Maple Leafs sign Borje Salming to a contract, knowing full well Harold's hatred for European players. Salming became an All-Star. Ballard's dead, and for much of his reign, so were the Leafs.

Poor health raises questions over Ballard's competency in running a hockey franchise.

Once one of the most penalized players in the league, Stan Mikita cleaned up his game enough to win the Lady Byng Trophy for gentlemanly play, twice. When he stayed out of the penalty box, he found time to win four scoring championships.

THE MIKITA EVOLUTION

HAVING BEEN LURED INTO THE ALLEYWAY UNDER THE PRETENSE OF
GETTING HIS FRONT 2 TEETH BACK, BOBBY WAS ANGERED BY THE
TOOTH FAIRY'S AUDACITY IN TRYING TO KNOCK OUT 2 MORE TEETH!

A spin of a roulette wheel decided whether Perreault would wear Buffalo blue or Canuck… yuk. Vancouver's long been known for it's lovely jerseys.

KNOWN FOR HIS GREAT DEKES, GILBERT PERREAULT'S MOST FAMOUS MOVE WAS AVOIDING HAVING TO WEAR THOSE VANCOUVER JERSEYS

Darryl Sittler had a dream night as he lit up the Boston net for 6 goals and a NHL record 10 points on February 7, 1976. The newly re-acquired Gerry Cheevers was spared the debacle, as coach Don Cherry mercilessly left rookie goalkeeper Dan Reece in for the duration of his worst nightmare.

Ex-president of the Player's Association, Alan Eagleson jailed for numerous offenses during his reign.

PROTECTING OUR ENDANGERED SPECIES

Instigator Esa Tikkanen.

an·tag·o·nize
to incur the
dislike of;
make an
enemy of
i.e ──→

IN THE LONG HISTORY OF THE NHLPA,
THESE TWO FIGURES REPRESENT THE TITLE BEST.

PLAYERS
TED LINDSAY – FOUNDING MEMBER

ASS.
ALAN EAGLESON

Two serious concussions shortened Pat LaFontaine's brilliant career.

While it's common for players to don multiple club uniforms during their hockey careers, it's rare to find any that have assumed the colours of three different nations. But nobody blamed Peter Stastny for turning the hat trick. After beginning his international career with Czechoslovakia, he pulled on a Canadian jersey in 1984 following his defection to Quebec from the communist nation. Then a decade later he completed the cycle by suiting up for his native Slovakia after it had become an independent nation.

Mario Lemieux is sidelined with a hip injury. The ailment to the other Penguins is anybody's guess.

Brian Leetch's plus-minus rating is less than spectacular during 97-98 season.

Vancouver was no Boardwalk for Mark Messier. At the time he received more critical acclaim for his commercials than for his hockey.

123

The notorious Tonya Harding would seem to be a perfect replacement for Marty McSorley, who was suspended for a sticking incident on Donald Brashear.

John Henry Williams has his father placed in cryonic suspension.

Good friends Paul Kariya and Teemu Selanne take less money to play on a contender together, but injuries and poor play put an end to the "free" agency experience.

Alexei Yashin reneges on the remainder of a million dollar donation when Ottawa's National Arts Center refuses to pay fees to Alexei's parents.

What is it with Ottawa players? Daigle, Yashin, Emery and now Heater.

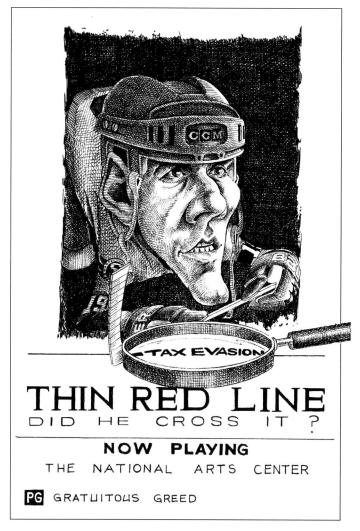

Officials were so worried about Avery's antics, they missed
the worst infraction of all - Jagr's post-season facial grooming.

It's bad enough when Avery pulled his antics on
Marty Brodeur, but when he shot his mouth off
about Canadian sweetheart, Elisha Cuthbert, it was
time to call in Jack Bauer.

The Richard riot was an ugly, ugly event both on the ice and off. On the lighter side league president Clarence Campbell got a souvenir pair of suspenders.

CAPTAIN CRUNCH ISN'T JUST A CEREAL.

During the 70's Boston and Philadelphia built their championship teams on big tough hockey. They were intimidating! Oh, they had skill and goaltending, but you don't earn nicknames like the Big Bad Bruins and the Broad Street Bullies by playing like choirboys.

The legendary Gordie Howe used intimidation in his game as well and it was at least partially due to his being ambidextrous. He could shoot an elbow from his left side or his right and this gave him the extra ice to use his other formidable skills. Twice during the 2007 playoffs Anaheim's Chris Pronger took a page out of the Howe playbook and used his elbows to create extra space. Unfortunately for Chris, the extra space was for the opposition when his 6'6 frame was suspended. (Obviously Chris hasn't learned Howe's fine art of discreetness). The tactics worked however, as the Senators looked apprehensive throughout the finals, perhaps worried where the next big hit would come from. The Ducks won in five games.

THE NEW CHAMP!

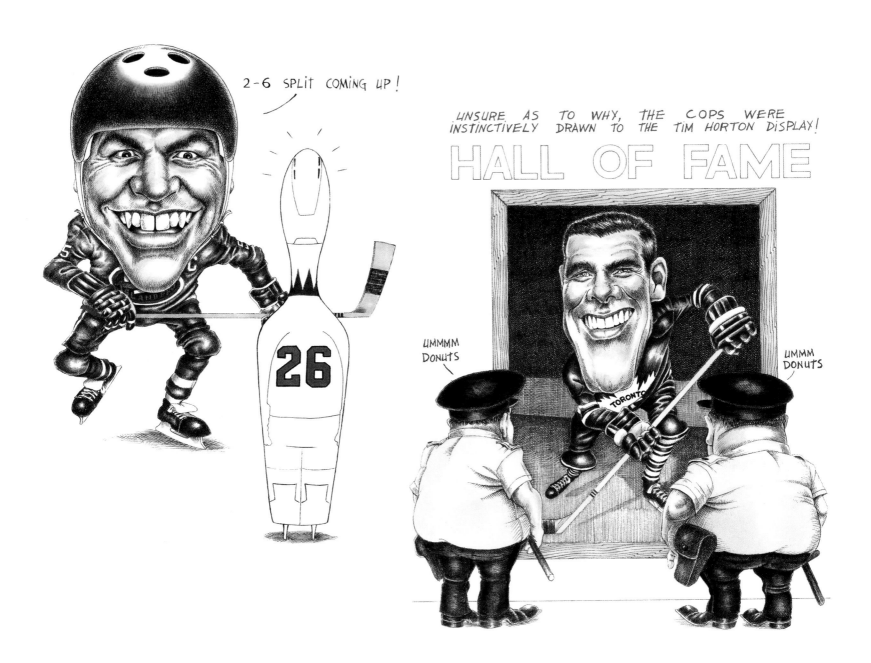

Larry Robinson's physical play was an even bigger factor in his number being retired than his offence.

"I'm going to have to find a line between being mean and taking penalties."
- Chris Chelios

UNLIKE DEER, CHELIOS VICTIMS WERE NEVER OUT OF SEASON

Cam Neely was born to be a Big Bad Bruin, while instigators like Claude Lemieux were born to get under his skin, but b-b-baulked at dropping the gloves.

Mark Messier.

At his peak, Rick Tocchet was a one man wrecking crew.

Darcy Tucker hits Mike Peca with a late, low check during the 2002 playoffs.

Mike Peca and Mats Sundin.

Chris Pronger becomes the first defenseman since Bobby Orr to be awarded league MVP in 2000.

ADAM'S FOOTE

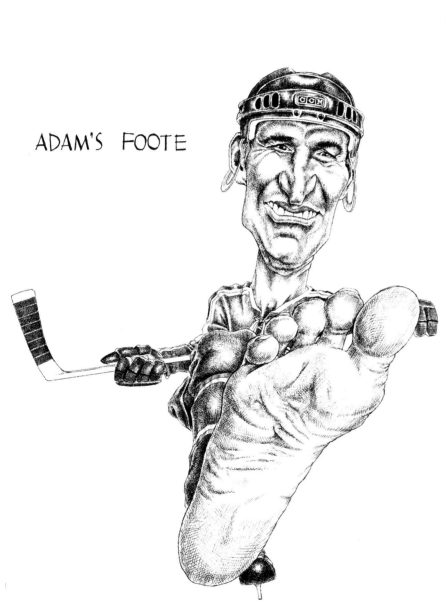

STAR LIGHT
STAR BRIGHT
FIRST STAR
I NAIL TONITE

Tie Domi was the obvious sparring partner for Zdeno Chara, but it was Brian McCabe, doing his best impersonation of a rag doll, who swung it out with him.

Not only a sugary cereal, the term 'Captain Crunch' would describe a select few hockey players known for their outstanding leadership and their ability to change a game with a devastating body check. One of the most notable is Hall of Famer Scott Stevens. Stevens who captained in New Jersey for over a decade, was notorious for delivering huge open ice hits, especially in key moments. Forwards cutting through the middle were best to keep their heads up or risk the consequences. Ask Eric Lindros or Paul Kariya about that, though you may have to repeat the question several times.

Dion Phaneuf.

ANYTHING YOU CAN DO, I CAN DO BETTER.

During the 1960's the Chicago Blackhawks boasted the NHL's two best players in Bobby Hull and Stan Mikita. By 1960, Hull was already an Art Ross and goal-scoring champion, while Mikita was known for his stick work, although not always in a good way.

In '61, Stan made an accidental discovery using a cracked blade. It would become known as the banana-curve and it wreaked havoc with the puck, causing it to curve and dip on the way to the goal. The pair experimented with the curvature of their blades in practice and games and it only added to the repertoire of the two future Hall of Famers, while also adding new creases on opposing goaltenders mask-less faces, either from stitches or stress lines.

From 1960-1968, the pair combined for seven scoring championships as well as pulling in four consecutive Hart Trophies as MVP. The best part was that they each anchored their own line, proving that they didn't need to play together to be dominant and anything one could do the other could do better.

141

With his speed, big shot and a severely curved blade, Bobby Hull can take a lot of credit for the emergence of the goalie mask during the 60's.

Al MacInnis can take at least as much credit for the bulking up of the rest of the goaltender's equipment. "You try to squeeze a little more Charmin in the pads when you face him."
– Ex-goalie Kevin Hodson.

Frank may be the only Mahovlich in the Hall of Fame, but 6'5" Peter overshadowed his older brother by recording the pair's only two 100 point seasons.

Doug Harvey's teammate Jacques Plante knitted tuques before eventually giving in to more protective headgear, but Doug never wore anything that masked his brilliance or hindered his on ice vision. He was the gauge by which all defensemen were measured, winning 7 Norris trophies in 8 years.

Orr won 8 in a row, fulfilling Harry Howell's 1967 prophecy " I might as well enjoy it now (Norris trophy), because I suspect it's going to belong to Bobby Orr from now on." Brad Park had to settle for runner up six times.

Kevin Lowe was the Oilers defensive anchor, but it was Paul Coffey who got the records and Norris trophies.

Tentime Stanley Cup champion, Jean Beliveau, was offered Canada's Governor General position but turned it down due to family commitments. Instead Canada ended up with Adrian Clarkson Presents and no off switch!

CANADA'S GOVERNOR GENERAL

WHAT COULD HAVE BEEN

REALITY

Henri Richard breaks Beliveau's and Cournoyer's record for playing on the most Stanley Cup winners with 11.

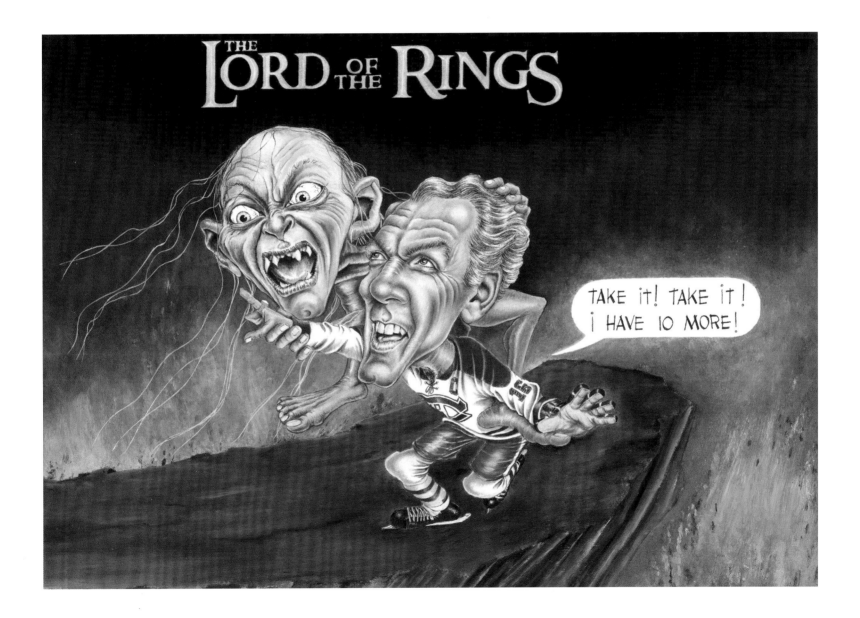

The Creation of Adam masterpiece is to the Sistine Chapel Ceiling as Bobby Orr was to the NHL.

If as the saying goes, imitation is the sincerest form of flattery, Raymond Bourque, Paul Coffey and Brian Leetch are paying a heck of a compliment to the incomparable Bobby Orr.

Mark Messier:

Eric Lindros patterned his game after his idol. Although he was bigger and stronger than the Moose, he lacked his leadership skills and wasn't as durable or colorful.

Martin Brodeur followed in his dad's footsteps. His father Denis, a renowned photographer, won a bronze medal playing in goal for Canada in the 1956 Olympics. Martin one-upped his dad by taking home gold in 2002.

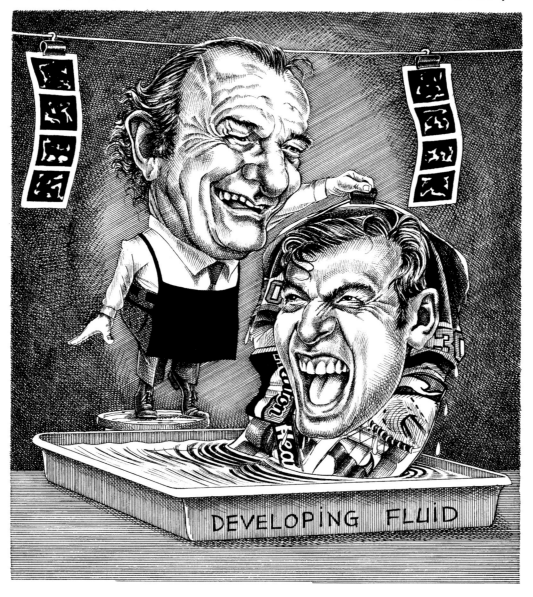

Peter Forsberg and Milan Hejduk.

When an opponent faced Colorado, they picked their poison. If Sakic didn't kill you, Forsberg did. They each led the playoffs in scoring twice. In 2001 Joe was MVP, while Peter had his turn in 2003. Sakic won a Conn Smythe, Forsberg won an Art Ross. They even took turns winning Olympic Gold, with Canada victorious in 2002, and Sweden in '06. Of course Forsberg has another gold from '94, but who's counting...

SPLAT

FORGOT THE PUCKIN DUCK!

BANG
BANG
BANG

Who's more valuable, the passer or the shooter? Crosby was MVP in 2007. Ovechkin equaled and then surpassed that with MVPs in 2008 and 2009.

THE MISSING SCORING LINK